DANIIL KARABUT

Teen Muscle

The Ultimate Bodybuilding Guide for Young Athletes

First edition

This book was professionally typeset on Reedsy.
Find out more at reedsy.com

"The only bad workout is the one that didn't happen."

Unknown

Contents

Preface

Bodybuilding has been a popular form of exercise for decades, and it continues to grow in popularity among teenagers. This book is intended to provide a comprehensive guide to bodybuilding for teenagers, focusing on safe and effective practices.

As a personal trainer and bodybuilding enthusiast, I've seen firsthand the benefits of bodybuilding for teenagers. Improved strength, endurance, and overall fitness can provide teenagers with numerous physical and mental benefits, from increased confidence to improved sports performance.

This book will cover everything from nutrition and workout plans to mental toughness and injury prevention. I hope this guide will help teenagers achieve their fitness goals safely and effectively while instilling healthy habits and practices that can be maintained throughout adulthood.

Remember that bodybuilding is a journey, not a destination. It requires dedication, commitment, and hard work, but the rewards are worthwhile. I hope this guide will inspire and motivate teenagers to achieve their fitness goals and maintain a healthy and active lifestyle for years.

Acknowledgement

I want to express my sincere gratitude to all those who contributed to developing this bodybuilding guide for teenagers.

First and foremost, I want to thank my family for their unwavering support and encouragement throughout writing this book. Their love and support motivated me to see this project through to completion.

I would also like to thank my colleagues in the fitness industry, who provided valuable insights and feedback throughout the development of this guide. Their knowledge and expertise were invaluable in shaping the content of this book.

Finally, I want to express my appreciation to all the teenagers passionate about bodybuilding and improving their fitness. Your dedication and commitment inspire me to continue sharing my knowledge and experience to help you achieve your fitness goals.

Thank you all for your contributions to this project. I hope this guide will provide a valuable resource for teenagers interested in bodybuilding and help them achieve their fitness goals safely and effectively.

Introduction: Why Bodybuilding is Important for Teenagers

Bodybuilding is a physical activity that involves resistance training and weightlifting to build muscle and strength. For many teenagers, bodybuilding may seem like a sport reserved for adults or professional athletes. However, bodybuilding can be an excellent way for teenagers to improve their physical and mental health, gain confidence, and achieve their fitness goals.

One of the main benefits of bodybuilding for teenagers is the physical improvements that come with regular exercise. By lifting weights and engaging in resistance training, teenagers can increase their muscle mass and improve their strength and endurance. This can lead to better athletic performance in other sports and activities and improved overall health and fitness.

In addition to the physical benefits, bodybuilding can also have a positive impact on mental health. Teenagers who exercise regularly, including bodybuilding, may experience reduced stress and anxiety, improved self-esteem and confidence, and better mood and cognitive function.

Furthermore, bodybuilding can provide teenagers with a sense of discipline and motivation. Developing a regular workout routine and committing to a healthy lifestyle can help teenagers build self-discipline and a strong work ethic that can benefit them in other areas, such as academics and career goals.

In this bodybuilding guide for teenagers, we will explore the science of muscle building, the importance of proper nutrition and exercise, and provide practical advice for creating a customized workout plan. Whether you are an experienced athlete or just starting, this guide will provide you with the knowledge and tools to build a robust and healthy body and mind through bodybuilding.

The Science of Muscle Building

Muscle building is a complex process involving various biological and physiological factors. Understanding the science behind muscle growth is critical to developing an effective bodybuilding routine and achieving your fitness goals.

At its core, muscle building is a process of cellular adaptation. During resistance training, such as weightlifting or bodyweight exercises, you create tiny tears in your muscle fibers. Your body then responds to these tears by repairing the damaged threads and adding new muscle tissue.

This process is known as muscle hypertrophy and is influenced by various factors, including genetics, age, sex, and hormone levels. Testosterone, for example, is a hormone that plays a crucial role in muscle growth and is naturally more abundant in males than females.

In addition to hormones, nutrition is a critical factor in muscle building. Consuming enough protein is essential for muscle growth, as proteins are the building blocks of muscle tissue. Carbohydrates and fats are also crucial for providing the energy needed for exercise and muscle repair.

Regular resistance training that progressively increases in intensity over time is essential to maximize muscle growth. This can be achieved through various exercises, including compound movements like squats and deadlifts and isolation exercises like bicep curls and leg extensions.

As you continue challenging your muscles with progressive resistance, your body will respond by building more muscle tissue and improving your overall strength and fitness.

Short Story:

As a teenager, I was always interested in fitness and sports. I played on my school's basketball team and loved to lift weights in my spare time. However, despite my dedication to exercise, my muscle-building progress was slow and frustrating.

It wasn't until I began to study the science of muscle building that I realized I was missing some crucial factors in my workout routine. By learning about the importance of proper nutrition, progressive resistance, and exercise variety, I developed a more effective bodybuilding routine that helped me achieve my fitness goals.

As a personal trainer and bodybuilding enthusiast, I hope to share my knowledge and experience with other teenagers interested in bodybuilding. Any teenager can build a robust and healthy body through bodybuilding by understanding the science behind muscle growth and applying that knowledge to their workout routine.

Nutrition for Teen Bodybuilders

Nutrition is a critical component of bodybuilding, and teenagers who engage in regular resistance training require a balanced and nutritious diet to support muscle growth and overall health. Proper nutrition can help teens build muscle, increase strength, and improve athletic performance.

One of the most important macronutrients for bodybuilding is protein. Protein is essential for muscle growth and repair and should make up a significant portion of a teen bodybuilder's diet. Good protein sources include lean meats, eggs, dairy products, and plant-based sources like beans and lentils.

Carbohydrates are also crucial for bodybuilding, providing the energy needed to perform resistance training exercises. Complex carbohydrates like whole grains, fruits, and vegetables are preferred over simple carbohydrates like sugar and processed foods.

Healthy fats, such as those in nuts, seeds, and avocados, are also crucial for bodybuilding. Fats provide energy and help the body absorb specific vitamins and minerals necessary for muscle growth.

In addition to macronutrients, vitamins, and minerals are critical for overall health and muscle building. Teen bodybuilders should aim to consume various nutrient-dense foods to ensure they are getting enough of these essential vitamins and minerals.

Proper hydration is also crucial for bodybuilding, as water is essential for transporting nutrients and maintaining cellular function. Teen bodybuilders should aim to drink plenty of water throughout the day, especially before and after workouts.

It's also essential for teen bodybuilders to avoid unhealthy habits like skipping meals or overeating, as these can negatively impact muscle growth and overall health.

Teen bodybuilders can support their muscle growth and improve their overall health and fitness by following a balanced and nutritious diet rich in protein, carbohydrates, healthy fats, and micronutrients.

Protein:

- Chicken breast
- Turkey breast
- Lean beef
- Eggs
- Low-fat dairy products (milk, yogurt, cottage cheese)
- Tuna fish
- Salmon
- Lentils
- Chickpeas
- Quinoa

Carbohydrates:

- Whole grain bread and pasta
- Brown rice

- Sweet potatoes
- Oatmeal
- Fruits (bananas, berries, apples, etc.)
- Vegetables (spinach, broccoli, kale, carrots, etc.)

Healthy Fats:

- Nuts (almonds, walnuts, peanuts, etc.)
- Seeds (chia, flax, pumpkin, etc.)
- Avocado
- Olive oil
- Coconut oil

Micronutrients:

- Dark leafy greens (spinach, kale, collard greens, etc.)
- Berries (blueberries, strawberries, raspberries, etc.)
- Citrus fruits (oranges, grapefruit, lemons, etc.)
- Whole grains (brown rice, quinoa, oats, etc.)
- Legumes (lentils, beans, peas, etc.)
- Low-fat dairy (milk, cheese, yogurt, etc.)
- Lean proteins (chicken, turkey, fish, etc.)

Hydration:

- Water
- Herbal tea
- Coconut water
- Low-sugar sports drinks

Teenage bodybuilders must consume a balanced and varied diet that includes all these food groups. They should aim to eat several small meals throughout the day to provide their bodies with a steady supply of nutrients and energy. Additionally, they should avoid sugary and processed foods as much as possible and opt for whole, nutrient-dense foods instead.

Creating a Workout Plan

Creating a workout plan is an essential part of bodybuilding for teenagers. A well-designed workout plan can help teens achieve their fitness goals, build muscle, and improve overall health and wellness. Here are some steps to follow when creating a workout plan for teenage bodybuilders:

1. Determine Your Fitness Goals: The first step in creating a workout plan is determining your fitness goals. Are you looking to build muscle mass? Improve strength? Increase endurance? Once you know your fitness goals clearly, you can tailor your workout plan accordingly.
2. Choose Your Exercises: The next step is to choose exercises to help you achieve your fitness goals. A good workout plan should include various activities targeting different muscle groups. Compound exercises like squats, deadlifts, bench presses, and pull-ups are practical for building strength and muscle mass. In contrast, isolation exercises like bicep curls and leg extensions can help to target specific muscle groups.
3. Determine the Frequency of Your Workouts: The frequency of your workouts will depend on your fitness goals and experience level. Beginners may start with 2-3 workouts

per week, while more experienced bodybuilders may train up to 5-6 times weekly. It's essential to give your body time to rest and recover between workouts, so include rest days in your workout plan.

4. Set Your Reps and Sets: Reps and sets refer to the number of repetitions and locations of each exercise you perform. This will depend on your fitness goals and experience level. For muscle building, a standard guideline is to complete 8-12 reps per set, with 3-4 sets per exercise.

5. Determine Your Rest Periods: Rest periods are the time you take between sets and exercises. For muscle building, taking 1-2 minutes of rest between sets is typically recommended to allow your muscles to recover.

6. Include Cardiovascular Exercise: While resistance training is essential for building muscle, cardiovascular exercise is necessary for overall health and fitness. Including a cardiovascular activity in your workout plan, such as running or cycling, can improve your endurance and cardiovascular health.

7. Track Your Progress: Tracking your progress is essential to staying motivated and progressing toward your fitness goals. Keep track of the weights you lift, the number of reps and sets you perform, and how your body feels after each workout.

Creating a workout plan takes time and effort, but it's an essential part of bodybuilding for teenagers.

Here are some examples of a workout plan for teenage bodybuilders:

Workout Plan 1 - Full-Body Workout (3 days per week): Day 1:

- Barbell Squats: 3 sets of 10 reps
- Barbell Bench Press: 3 sets of 10 reps
- Barbell Rows: 3 sets of 10 reps
- Dumbbell Shoulder Press: 3 sets of 10 reps
- Plank: Hold for 30 seconds; repeat three times

Day 2:

- Deadlifts: 3 sets of 10 reps
- Pull-Ups: 3 sets of 10 reps
- Dumbbell Lunges: 3 sets of 10 reps (each leg)
- Dumbbell Bicep Curls: 3 sets of 10 reps
- Hanging Leg Raises: 3 sets of 10 reps

Day 3:

- Barbell Squats: 3 sets of 10 reps
- Barbell Overhead Press: 3 sets of 10 reps
- Dumbbell Bench Press: 3 sets of 10 reps
- Barbell Rows: 3 sets of 10 reps
- Plank: Hold for 30 seconds; repeat three times

Workout Plan 2 - Upper Body/Lower Body Split (4 days per week):
Day 1 (Upper Body):

- Barbell Bench Press: 4 sets of 8 reps
- Barbell Rows: 4 sets of 8 reps
- Dumbbell Shoulder Press: 4 sets of 8 reps
- Pull-Ups: 3 sets of 8 reps
- Dumbbell Bicep Curls: 3 sets of 10 reps

Day 2 (Lower Body):

- Barbell Squats: 4 sets of 8 reps
- Deadlifts: 4 sets of 8 reps
- Leg Press: 4 sets of 10 reps
- Leg Extensions: 3 sets of 10 reps
- Leg Curls: 3 sets of 10 reps

Day 3 (Rest Day)
Day 4 (Upper Body):

- Dumbbell Bench Press: 4 sets of 8 reps
- Lat Pulldowns: 4 sets of 8 reps
- Dumbbell Rows: 4 sets of 8 reps
- Barbell Bicep Curls: 3 sets of 10 reps
- Tricep Pushdowns: 3 sets of 10 reps

Day 5 (Lower Body):

- Barbell Lunges: 4 sets of 8 reps (each leg)
- Romanian Deadlifts: 4 sets of 8 reps
- Calf Raises: 4 sets of 10 reps
- Leg Press: 3 sets of 10 reps
- Leg Curls: 3 sets of 10 reps

Day 6-7 (Rest Days)
Note: Adjust the weight, reps, and sets based on your experience level and fitness goals. Additionally, warm up properly before beginning any workout, and cool down and stretch afterward to prevent injury.

Essential Exercises for Teen Bodybuilders

Building a solid and muscular physique requires resistance training exercises targeting multiple muscle groups. As a teenage bodybuilder, you must include various activities in your workout routine to ensure you're targeting all major muscle groups and achieving your fitness goals. Here are some vital practices for teen bodybuilders:

1. Barbell Squats are among the most effective exercises for building lower body strength and muscle mass. The barbell squat targets the quadriceps, hamstrings, and glutes.
2. Deadlifts: Deadlifts are a compound exercise that targets the entire posterior chain, including the hamstrings, glutes, and lower back. Deadlifts are essential for building overall strength and power.
3. Barbell Bench Press: The barbell bench press is a classic exercise that targets the chest, shoulders, and triceps. Performing the activity properly is essential to avoid injury and maximize results.
4. Pull-Ups: Pull-ups are a bodyweight exercise that targets the back, biceps, and shoulders. Pull-ups can be challenging but essential for building upper body strength and

muscular development.

5. Dumbbell Shoulder Press: The dumbbell shoulder press is an effective exercise for building strength and mass. It targets the deltoid muscles, triceps, and upper chest.

6. Barbell Rows: Barbell rows are a compound exercise that targets the back muscles, including the lats and rhomboids. They are an essential exercise for building a solid and well-developed back.

7. Lunges: Lunges are excellent for building lower body strength and muscle mass. They target the quadriceps, hamstrings, and glutes and can be performed with or without weights.

8. Dumbbell Bicep Curls: Bicep curls are isolation exercises targeting the biceps. They can be performed with dumbbells, barbells, or resistance bands.

9. Tricep Pushdowns: Tricep pushdowns are an isolation exercise that targets the triceps. They can be performed with a cable machine or resistance bands.

10. Planks: Planks are an excellent exercise for building core strength and stability. They target the entire core, including the abs, obliques, and lower back.

Proper Lifting Techniques

Lifting weights can be an effective way to build muscle and improve overall fitness, but it's essential to use proper lifting techniques to avoid injury and maximize results. Here are some tips for using proper lifting techniques:

1. Warm Up Properly: Before beginning any weightlifting exercise, it's essential to warm up your muscles with some light cardiovascular conditioning and dynamic stretching. This will help to increase blood flow and prepare your muscles for the upcoming workout.
2. Use Proper Form: Proper form is essential for lifting weights safely and effectively. Use proper posture and alignment and engage the appropriate muscle groups for each exercise. Avoid arching your back or using momentum to lift weights, as this can unnecessarily strain your muscles and joints.
3. Use a Proper Grip: Use a comfortable and secure grip for proper form. For example, when lifting weights with a barbell, use an overhand grip with your hands slightly wider than shoulder-width apart.
4. Breathe Properly: Proper breathing is essential for lifting weights safely and effectively. Breathe in through your

nose and out through your mouth, and exhale on the effort of each exercise. For example, exhale when lifting the weight and inhale when lowering it.

5. Use Proper Weight: Too much weight can strain your muscles and joints unnecessarily, while too little weight may not provide enough resistance to challenge your muscles. Choose a weight that is appropriate for your experience level and fitness goals.

6. Progress Gradually: It's important to progress gradually when lifting weights rather than raising the heaviest weight possible immediately. Gradually increase the weight and intensity over time to avoid injury and ensure consistent progress.

7. Cool Down and Stretch: After completing your weightlifting workout, cool down with light cardiovascular exercise and static stretching. This will help to prevent muscle soreness and promote flexibility.

Tracking Progress

Tracking your progress is essential to bodybuilding, as it allows you to monitor your progress toward your fitness goals and adjust your workout routine as needed. Here are some tips for tracking your progress as a teenage bodybuilder:

1. Keep a Workout Journal: A workout journal is a great way to track your progress. Write down the exercises you perform, the weights you lift, the number of sets and reps you complete, and any notes about how you feel during and after each workout.

2. Take Progress Pictures: Taking progress pictures can be a great way to track your progress over time visually. Take photos from the same angles every few weeks to see how your body changes.

3. Use Body Measurements: Body measurements, such as waist circumference, bicep circumference, and body fat percentage, can help you track your progress toward your fitness goals. Measure yourself every few weeks and compare your measurements over time.

4. Set Achievable Goals: Setting achievable goals is vital for staying motivated and tracking progress. Set short-term and long-term goals, and track your progress towards each

one.

5. Use Fitness Apps: There are many fitness apps available that can help you track your progress. These apps can track your workouts, provide exercise suggestions, and help you stay motivated and accountable.

6. Listen to Your Body: Listening to your body when tracking progress is essential. Pay attention to how your body feels during and after workouts, and adjust your workout routine as needed to avoid injury and maximize results.

You can stay motivated and adjust your workout routine by tracking your progress as a teenage bodybuilder. Remember to set achievable goals, use various tracking methods, and listen to your body to ensure consistent progress toward your fitness goals.

Here's an example of a workout journal entry:

Date: March 15, 2023

Workout: Upper Body (Day 1)

Exercises:

- Barbell Bench Press: 4 sets of 8 reps (75 kg)
- Barbell Rows: 4 sets of 8 reps (75 kg)
- Dumbbell Shoulder Press: 4 sets of 10 reps (25 kg)
- Pull-Ups: 3 sets of 8 reps (bodyweight)
- Dumbbell Bicep Curls: 3 sets of 10 reps (20 kg)

Notes:

- Felt good during the workout and had good energy
- Increased weight for bench press and rows by 5 lbs from last

week
- Felt a good burn in the biceps during the curls
- I struggled with the previous set of pull-ups; I will try to increase reps next week

You can monitor your progress and adjust your workout routine by keeping track of the exercises, sets, reps, and weights used in each workout. Additionally, including notes about how you feel during and after each workout can help you identify areas for improvement and stay motivated.

Rest and Recovery

Rest and recovery are essential components of bodybuilding for teenagers. While it's important to engage in resistance training and cardiovascular exercise to build muscle and improve overall fitness, giving your body time to rest and recover between workouts is equally important. Here are some tips for rest and recovery as a teenage bodybuilder:

1. Get Enough Sleep: Sleep is essential for muscle growth and recovery. Aim for 7-9 hours of sleep per night to allow your body to recover from workouts and regenerate muscle tissue.
2. Take Rest Days: Rest days are essential for giving your body time to recover and prevent injury. Plan rest days into your workout routine and avoid engaging in strenuous physical activity on these days.
3. Practice Active Recovery: While rest is essential, active recovery is also significant to promote blood flow and muscle regeneration. Light cardiovascular exercise, stretching, and foam rolling are all effective forms of active recovery.
4. Eat a Balanced Diet: Proper nutrition is essential for muscle growth and recovery. Be sure to eat a balanced diet with plenty of protein, complex carbohydrates, and healthy fats.

5. Stay Hydrated: Drinking enough water is essential for muscle recovery and overall health. Aim for 8-10 glasses of water daily, and drink more if you're engaging in strenuous physical activity.

6. Manage Stress: Stress can hurt muscle growth and recovery. Manage stress through techniques like meditation, deep breathing, or yoga.

7. Listen to Your Body: It's essential to listen to your body and take rest and recovery days as needed. If you're tired, sore, or unmotivated, it may be a sign that your body needs rest.

Overcoming Plateaus

As a teenage bodybuilder, you may experience plateaus where your progress stalls and you no longer see improvements in strength or muscle growth. Here are some tips for overcoming plateaus and getting back on track with your fitness goals:

1. Change Up Your Workout Routine: If you've been following the same workout routine for an extended period, it may be time to switch things up. Try incorporating new exercises, increasing the weight or reps, or changing the order of your activities to shock your muscles and promote growth.
2. Increase Your Intensity: If you've been lifting the same weight for the same number of reps for a while, it may be time to increase the intensity of your workouts. Add more weight, decrease rest time between sets, or incorporate supersets or drop locations to challenge your muscles.
3. Take a Break: Sometimes, taking a break from your workout routine can help you overcome a plateau. Take a week off lifting weights or engage in a different form of exercise, such as yoga or swimming, to give your muscles a break and return stronger.
4. Adjust Your Nutrition: Proper nutrition is essential for muscle growth and recovery. If you're not seeing progress

in your fitness goals, it may be time to adjust your diet. Ensure you're consuming enough protein, healthy fats, and complex carbohydrates.

5. Focus on Form: Sometimes, minor adjustments can make a big difference in your results. Use proper form and technique during exercises to ensure you target the right muscles and maximize your results.

6. Get Enough Rest: Rest and recovery are essential for muscle growth and recovery. Ensure you get enough sleep, take rest days, and engage in active recovery to optimize muscle growth.

Supplements for Teen Bodybuilders

While proper nutrition and exercise are the foundation of any effective bodybuilding program, some teenagers may consider adding supplements to their routines to enhance their performance and achieve their fitness goals. Here are some accessories that may be beneficial for teenage bodybuilders:

1. Protein Powder: Protein powder is a popular supplement for bodybuilders of all ages. It's a convenient and easy way to ensure that you're consuming enough protein to support muscle growth and recovery. Look for a high-quality protein powder that contains all essential amino acids.

2. Creatine: Creatine is a natural compound found in the body that produces energy during high-intensity exercise. Supplementing with creatine can help to increase muscle mass and strength and improve exercise performance.

3. Beta-Alanine: Beta-alanine is an amino acid used to produce carnosine, which helps to buffer lactic acid in the muscles during exercise. Supplementing with beta-alanine may improve exercise performance and delay fatigue.

4. Caffeine is a natural stimulant that can improve energy levels and focus during workouts. It can also help to

increase metabolism and burn fat. However, it's essential to consume caffeine in moderation and avoid consuming it close to bedtime.

5. Omega-3 Fatty Acids: Omega-3 fatty acids are essential fats that play a role in muscle growth and recovery. They can also help to reduce inflammation and improve overall health. Look for a high-quality fish oil supplement that contains EPA and DHA.

It's important to note that while supplements can be a helpful addition to a bodybuilding program, they should not replace proper nutrition and exercise. Additionally, it's essential to consult with a healthcare professional before starting any new supplement regimen, particularly if you have any underlying health conditions.

Training at Home vs. in a Gym

Regarding bodybuilding, there are pros and cons to training at home versus in a gym. Here are some considerations for each option:

Training at Home:

Pros:

- Convenience: One of the most significant advantages of training at home is convenience. You can work out anytime without worrying about gym hours, waiting for equipment, or commuting to a gym.
- Cost Savings: Training at home can save you money on gym membership fees and transportation costs.
- Privacy: Some people prefer working out at home without worrying about being judged by others or feeling self-conscious.

Cons:

- Limited Equipment: Unless you have a fully equipped home gym, you may not have access to all the necessary equipment to target all major muscle groups and achieve your fitness goals.

- Lack of Motivation: Without the social environment of a gym, it can be easy to lose motivation and not push yourself as hard during workouts.
- Distractions: Working out at home can be distracting, especially if you have children, pets, or other household responsibilities that demand your attention.

Training in a Gym:
Pros:

- Access to Equipment: A gym typically has a wide range of equipment, including machines, free weights, and cardio equipment, to target all major muscle groups and achieve your fitness goals.
- Social Environment: A gym can provide a social environment that can be motivating and energizing. You can meet other like-minded individuals, make friends, and push yourself harder during workouts.
- Professional Guidance: Many gyms have personal trainers to guide exercise technique, proper form, and workout routines.

Cons:

- Cost: Gym membership fees can be expensive, especially if you choose a high-end gym or personal training sessions.
- Time Constraints: Going to a gym requires you to schedule your workouts around gym hours and your schedule.
- Crowds: Depending on the gym and the time of day, you may have to wait for equipment or deal with groups.

Whether you train at home or in a gym depends on your preferences, budget, and fitness goals. You may find that a combination of both options works best for you.

Mental Toughness for Teen Bodybuilders

In addition to physical strength and endurance, mental toughness is essential for success as a teenage bodybuilder. Here are some tips for developing mental toughness:

1. Set Clear Goals: Setting clear goals and tracking progress towards those goals can help to keep you motivated and focused. Ensure your goals are specific, measurable, achievable, relevant, and time-bound (SMART).
2. Push-Through Plateaus: Plateaus are a normal part of bodybuilding but can be frustrating. Use plateaus to challenge yourself and try new approaches to your workouts.
3. Visualize Success: Visualization techniques can help build mental toughness. Visualize yourself achieving your fitness goals and imagine the feeling of success.
4. Stay Positive: A positive mindset can help you push through tough workouts and overcome obstacles. Focus on the progress you've made and the improvements you're making rather than getting bogged down in setbacks.
5. Embrace Discomfort: Bodybuilding can be uncomfortable and challenging, but embracing discomfort can help you develop mental toughness. Push yourself out of your

comfort zone during workouts and embrace the feeling of accomplishment.

6. Learn from Setbacks: Setbacks are an inevitable part of bodybuilding but can also be an opportunity for growth. Use setbacks to learn from your mistakes and adjust your approach.

7. Stay Committed: Building mental toughness requires commitment and consistency. Stay committed to your fitness goals and remain consistent in your workouts and nutrition plan.

By developing mental toughness as a teenage bodybuilder, you can stay motivated, overcome challenges, and achieve your fitness goals. Remember to set clear goals, push through plateaus, visualize success, stay positive, embrace discomfort, learn from setbacks, and stay committed.

Staying Safe While Bodybuilding

While bodybuilding can be a safe and effective way to improve strength and overall fitness, it's essential to prioritize safety to avoid injury. Here are some tips for staying safe while bodybuilding:

1. Warm Up: Before starting any workout, it's essential to warm up to help prevent injury. This can include light cardio, dynamic stretching, and mobility exercises.
2. Use Proper Form: Proper form and technique are essential for preventing injury and maximizing results. If you're unsure how to perform an exercise in good condition, seek guidance from a personal trainer or fitness professional.
3. Increase weight Gradually: Adding too much weight too quickly can put you at risk for injury, so increase weight in small increments.
4. Wear Proper Gear: Wearing proper gear, such as supportive shoes, can help to prevent injury. Additionally, using weightlifting gloves can help to prevent calluses and blisters.
5. Listen to Your Body: It's essential to listen to your body and avoid pushing yourself too hard. If you feel pain or discomfort during a workout, stop immediately and seek

medical attention if necessary.

For example, I made the mistake of lifting too much weight too quickly during a bench press exercise, which resulted in a strained chest muscle. I learned the importance of gradually increasing weight and using proper form to avoid injury.

By prioritizing safety while bodybuilding, you can prevent injury and achieve your fitness goals safely and effectively. Remember to warm up, use proper form, increase weight gradually, wear appropriate gear, and listen to your body.

Bodybuilding for Sports Performance

While bodybuilding is often associated with aesthetic goals, it can also improve sports performance. Here are some ways that bodybuilding can enhance sports performance:

1. Strength: Building strength through resistance training can improve overall athletic performance, particularly in sports that require power, explosiveness, and agility.
2. Muscle Endurance: Building muscle endurance can help to delay fatigue and improve performance during longer-duration athletic events, such as distance running, soccer, or basketball.
3. Injury Prevention: Resistance training can help to strengthen muscles, tendons, and ligaments, which can help to prevent injuries and improve overall durability.
4. Flexibility: Incorporating stretching and mobility exercises into a bodybuilding program can improve overall flexibility and range of motion, enhancing sports performance.
5. Mental Toughness: Building mental toughness through bodybuilding can help athletes push through fatigue and discomfort during athletic events and remain focused and motivated.

When incorporating bodybuilding into a sports performance training program, it's essential to tailor the exercises and routines to the specific sport and the individual athlete's needs. For example, a football player may build upper body strength to improve his tackling ability. In contrast, a soccer player may focus on building lower body strength and endurance for sprinting and kicking power.

By incorporating bodybuilding into a sports performance training program, athletes can improve strength, endurance, injury prevention, flexibility, and mental toughness, ultimately improving their overall athletic performance.

Maintaining a Bodybuilding Lifestyle Beyond Teenage Years

As a teenage bodybuilder, it's essential to establish healthy habits and routines that can be maintained throughout adulthood. Here are some tips for maintaining a bodybuilding lifestyle beyond your teenage years:

1. Set Realistic Goals: Your fitness goals may change as you age. Set realistic goals that align with your current lifestyle and fitness level.

2. Adapt Your Workouts: As you age, it's crucial to adapt your workouts to avoid injury and accommodate changes in strength and flexibility. Focus on exercises that target major muscle groups, and incorporate more flexibility and mobility exercises to maintain range of motion.

3. Prioritize Recovery: Recovery becomes increasingly essential as you age. Get enough sleep, rest days, and active recovery to promote muscle growth and prevent injury.

4. Continue to Fuel Your Body: Proper nutrition is essential for maintaining a bodybuilding lifestyle. Adjusting your diet to accommodate the metabolism and overall health changes is vital as you age.

5. Seek Professional Guidance: As you age, seeking guidance

from a personal trainer or fitness professional may be helpful to ensure you're engaging in safe and effective exercise routines.

6. Stay Motivated: Maintaining a bodybuilding lifestyle requires commitment and motivation. Find ways to stay motivated, such as tracking progress, incorporating new exercises, or finding a workout buddy.

You can maintain a bodybuilding lifestyle well beyond your teenage years by prioritizing realistic goals, adapting your workouts, prioritizing recovery, continuing to fuel your body, seeking professional guidance, and staying motivated. Remember to prioritize overall health and safety and listen to your body as you age.

Conclusion

Bodybuilding can be an effective way for teenagers to improve strength, endurance, and overall fitness. By following a balanced nutrition plan, establishing a consistent workout routine, and prioritizing safety and recovery, teenage bodybuilders can achieve their fitness goals safely and effectively.

In addition to physical strength and endurance, mental toughness is essential for success as a teenage bodybuilder. By setting clear goals, pushing through plateaus, visualizing success, staying positive, embracing discomfort, learning from setbacks, and staying committed, teenage bodybuilders, can develop the mental toughness needed to achieve their fitness goals.

While bodybuilding may be associated with aesthetic goals, it can also be beneficial for improving sports performance and maintaining overall health and fitness throughout adulthood. By adapting workouts, prioritizing recovery, fueling the body, seeking professional guidance, and staying motivated, bodybuilders can maintain a healthy and active lifestyle beyond their teenage years.

Remember to prioritize safety, listen to your body, and seek guidance from healthcare professionals when necessary. With dedication and commitment, teenage bodybuilders can achieve their fitness goals and live a healthy and active lifestyle.

Made in the USA
Monee, IL
20 November 2024

70658254R00026